RECRUITING SUCKS...BUT
IT DOESN'T HAVE TO

RECRUITING SUCKS...BUT IT DOESN'T HAVE TO

BREAKING THROUGH THE MYTHS THAT GOT US HERE

STEVE LOWISZ

LIONCREST
PUBLISHING

RECRUITING SUCKS…BUT IT DOESN'T HAVE TO

Breaking Through the Myths That Got Us Here

ISBN   978-1-5445-0173-4 *Hardcover*

     978-1-5445-0172-7 *Paperback*

     978-1-5445-0171-0 *Ebook*

Dedicated to Cheryl—for encouraging me to share my experiences with others, so they learn from my mistakes and avoid their own.

CONTENTS

INTRODUCTION...9

1. MYTH #1:
    SKILLS ARE THE MOST IMPORTANT THING 17

2. MYTH #2:
    LINKEDIN IS THE END-ALL-BE-ALL SOURCE FOR RECRUITING.........39

3. MYTH #3:
    RECRUITERS DON'T NEED TO BE MARKETERS 61

4. MYTH #4:
    CANDIDATES ARE ONLY INTERESTED IN TITLES AND MONEY 77

5. MYTH #5:
    RECRUITERS ARE NOT RESPONSIBLE FOR THE QUALITY OF A HIRE ..91

6. MYTH #6:
    RECRUITERS WILL BE REPLACED BY TECHNOLOGY 103

CONCLUSION..111

ABOUT THE AUTHOR 115

INTRODUCTION

RECRUITING SUCKS

"People are our most important asset." We hear it all the time—because it's true. Most savvy business leaders understand the tremendous value of having the right people on a team. Everyone knows (or at least pretends they know) that "people power," "human capital," "the right people on the bus," etc., is the name of the game.

But the way in which we go about *recruiting* those people is all f****d up.

If that sounds harsh to you, consider the history of the modern recruiting industry, which emerged after World War II. It has been essentially the same for the past seventy-five years, from the way we interview candidates to the way we do our job descriptions.

Yes, the technology has changed, dramatically so. But the underlying process has not—and, as I argue in this book, it is a *broken* process.

We've used technology to speed up recruiting. But when you apply technology to an already broken process, are you really improving anything?

No. In fact, you are just speeding up failure, which is part of why **recruiting sucks...but it doesn't have to.**

Other industries have changed with the times. Yet recruiters are still using the same process we did in the 1940s. Worst of all, we *know* it's not working. But we keep doing the same thing and expecting a different result.

How do we know it's not working? Just look at the high employee turnover rate that so many companies are facing.

We've all heard the alarming stats about the cost of a mis-hire. According to Dr. Bradford Smart, author of *Topgrading*, a bad hire ends up costing a company somewhere between five and twenty-seven times the individual's salary.

Again, we all *know* this, whether we're an internal recruiter, a third-party agency, or in HR. We know the cost of turnover, the cost of recruiting a new candidate, the cost of an open position, and the potential cost of losing a client. We also know the devastating impact of a mis-hire on morale and performance of other employees.

We know all these consequences, and we understand that people are the most important asset—but we don't view recruiting through this lens.

Instead, we mistakenly view recruiting as a transaction.

HOW WE GOT HERE

In every industry and every role, there must be clear objectives. No one is arguing against that. But when it becomes all about the numbers, about the transaction, it gets in the way of what's most important. We can't forget that in recruiting, the most important thing is *relationships*.

Or, rather, it should be.

Unfortunately, all too often in the world of recruiting, we don't take the time or do the work to get to know the whole candidate, the full human being. We focus on the process, not the relationship. And then we wonder why we struggle.

If you're like most recruiters I speak to, you experience a good deal of frustration in your daily life. You feel like no matter how hard you try, you can't find enough candidates. Maybe you even take that frustration home with you.

I'm here to tell you: it doesn't have to be like this. There is a different way that will lead to different results and help you break free from this cycle.

But it means setting aside your old, ingrained habits. It means prioritizing relationships rather than process. Yes, process is important. But if **process gets in the way of progress, then it's the wrong process.**

This is where we recruiters have gotten it wrong time and again. We fail to look at the root cause of our issues: how we go about recruiting people.

Instead, we attach more and more Band-Aids to the problem. We get the wrong person for a job and then we reverse engineer the job description to fit the person. Or we tinker with the compensation, hoping to get a higher quality candidate.

But we never actually go back to the root and look at the fundamental question of how we should be finding and assessing candidates.

CONSIDER THE POSSIBILITY

What if, instead of being frustrated—instead of thinking that the problems you're facing in your industry are everyone else's fault—you began to see yourself as the person who could make the difference?

No doubt, the recruiting industry has several inherent structural problems, some of which are unlikely to change anytime soon. For one thing, it's still motivated by placements at any cost, especially in third-party agencies that work primarily off commission.

To make matters worse, as I touched on earlier, many recruiters know little to nothing about their candidates.

It wasn't until I experienced the recruiting industry as a *customer* that I realized just how bad it was. On the bright side, it was that very experience that set in motion my journey and led me to find my *own* solutions—and to share them now, twenty-four years later, in this book.

It all began when I was working as general sales manager of an office equipment dealership in metropolitan Detroit. I was tasked with recruiting new sales and service professionals in an effort to grow the business.

After calling up some recruiting firms and telling them what I was looking for, the basic skillset requirements, etc., they started sending me people. Boy, were these candidates terrible! It was like the recruiters hadn't even listened to me. They were just throwing stuff at the wall and seeing what stuck.

Eventually, I hired a couple of folks, but they didn't last long. Looking back, I realized I made the common mistake of hiring the "best of the worst."

Thankfully, I soon connected with a better firm out of Chicago, who seemed to actually listen to what I told them. They gave me a list of people whom they thought seemed right, but amazingly, encouraged me to do the recruiting part myself. They could see I knew what I was looking for and believed I had the right instincts to handle the task on my own.

So I picked up the phone and started to form relationships with the talent I wanted to bring to the company. I took them to lunch and out for drinks. In the end, I successfully recruited several great people myself, based on my outreach and the strength of our relationships.

Wow, I thought to myself. *I'm better at this than most recruiters!*

Looking back now, I see that this period of my life and career was foundational. My experiences as a recruiter *and* as a client of recruiters gave me a unique perspective and a rare vantage point in the industry.

Through those early years, through trial and error, I essentially created my own recruiting machine—but based off the relationship, not the transaction.

Nowadays, I'm known as an industry veteran and disruptor. But my insights are based on more than theory; I've lived and gone through it all myself. Moreover, I practice what I preach—I see how well this new recruiting process works on a daily basis.

If I had come to the industry from a more traditional path, I'm not sure I would have been able to see it through the fresh eyes that I did.

In a way, my youth and naivete allowed me to identify the myths that held the industry hostage—and still do.

THE MYTHS OF RECRUITING

It's a common saying in business: "cost, speed, quality—pick two." In other words, you can't have it all. It's an old-school way of thinking, but there's some validity to it. Recruiters, for example, have certainly sacrificed quality for speed.

But the truth is, you *can* have it all if you approach it in the right way. The "pick two" thing is a myth. And it's just one of many myths that have held back the recruiting industry for far too long.

In the following chapters, I am going to walk you through some of the many ways that this old-school, status quo mentality has kept the industry broken. I'll puncture these widespread misconceptions, and in their place, I'll put forth a groundbreaking *new* way of doing recruiting, from sourcing to interviewing to marketing.

Far from an abstract, philosophical discussion, I will provide practical, proven solutions for finding, developing, and maintaining top talent.

Yes, recruiting sucks...but it doesn't have to.

Chapter One

MYTH #1: SKILLS ARE THE MOST IMPORTANT THING

For his book *Hiring for Attitude,* Mark Murphy conducted a fascinating research study into why so many new hires fail so quickly. What he found was that only 11 percent of the time does it have to do with a lack of skill. Almost always, it's a matter of *behavior*. Among new hires who fail within eighteen months, 89 percent do so for what he calls "attitude."

Murphy's solution: hire for attitude, not skills. Skills can be learned with training.

Coming from a recruiting perspective, I'm inclined to

agree. I'm not suggesting we ignore skills entirely. But the fact of the matter is we *already* do a pretty great job of looking at skills, and we do it through every step of the recruiting process—from résumés to interviews to keyword searches.

The point is, yes, skills are important, but clearly, we've got that part covered. As recruiters, we are experts at identifying skills, which is why only 11 percent of new-hire failures fail for that reason! But what about the other 89 percent? What are we getting wrong? How are we letting this happen?

We must ask ourselves: how well do we even understand the candidates we are recruiting?

Could it be that we are not really seeing them at all?

THE THREE PARTS OF A HUMAN BEING

It is my contention that when we hire, we actually only hire for *one-third* of a person.

Each of us is made up of three parts: head, heart, and skills. But as recruiters, we are trained to dig into only the third piece. We barely get into candidates' heads. And their hearts? Forget about it. We're almost completely in the dark. We scrutinize candidates for their abilities to do what the job description asks of them, but the how and why behind what they do remains a mystery.

What would it look like if, instead of hiring for a fraction of a person, we took into consideration the totality of the human being?

In order to answer that question, we must first be clear on what exactly is meant by head, heart, and skills. It makes sense to start with the one we're already most comfortable with: skills.

SKILLS

What do we mean when we talk about skills? This one is easy to answer: does the candidate have the functional capacity to do the job? If they're an IT manager, do they have the skillset to be an IT manager? If they're an artist, do they have the skillset to be an artist?

When we hire for skills, we are trying to answer the question "*can* they do it?"

But there are other important questions, too: "*will* they do it?" (head) and "*why* will they do it?" (heart).

Foolishly, we focus on only the *can*. We put all our effort into looking at skills. Take, for example, job descriptions.

They say things like "ten years of experience required" or "fifteen years of experience required." It may seem harmless, but ask yourself: is "years of experience" *really* an important metric, or is it just the lens that we've been trained to use? **Does "years of experience" equal a skill?**

Many job descriptions operate on the assumption that it takes ten or fifteen years to attain such-and-such skills. But what if a fast learner mastered those skills in four years? I'll tell you what would happen: that person wouldn't even be in the running. Employers would miss out on a potential superstar.

How does that make any sense?

We exclude these high-potential candidates because of these stupid rules and the silly assumption that years of experience equals a skill. Instead, why not just ask what candidates actually have to accomplish in the job? Why not focus on the measurable *results* expected of them in the first sixty days, ninety days, etc.?

THE HEAD AND THE HEART

The second piece of a candidate to consider is the **head**. The head is about how the candidate is wired, the behaviors that are rooted in their innate needs. These are what make someone act and communicate a certain way. They also determine if the person needs to own a process versus having a team own a process.

But when we talk about the head, we are also talking about a candidate's cognitive ability, or the level of complexity they can manage in their position. Every job has a different cognitive threshold based on its complexity, and some people are better equipped than others to think and react quickly in complex situations.

Through both its behavioral and cognitive aspects, the head reveals all kinds of valuable information. It shows whether people are prone to be more independent or more collaborative; whether they enjoy high pressure and constant change or prefer a steady-state environment; whether they like to work within a clear framework or make their own framework.

Then there's the **heart**, which refers to someone's motivation. While behavior is the way we act—based on our inherent needs—the heart is about what's most important to us, based on our purpose. The heart is the *why* behind everything, and the *why* is probably the hardest aspect to identify in a candidate. It's simple to identify skills. It's a little more difficult to identify behaviors, but there are tools to help with that. But to really dig inside and figure out a candidate's *why* is not easy at all—which is why so many people don't do it.

THE PERFORMANCE BLUEPRINT™

The first step in a recruiting process is to understand what a hiring manager needs. As a recruiter, you must perform what is called an "intake session" to get this information. When I hold workshops for recruiters, I illustrate the common approach to an intake session by putting a complete job description on a screen behind me that describes the role. I'll ask the audience of 300 people, "What do you think you need to know about this job?"

I'll get the typical questions like these: How many years of experience do they need? What's the geographic area? How many people are on this person's team? Do they need a degree? These are all important questions. Yet, they are all practical and skills-based. Some aren't as relevant as we imagine. For example, did you know that when it comes to degrees and results, the correlation is 1 percent or less?

The old intake session is all about the job description. I prefer *not* to start with a job description. Typically when a recruiter receives one, they ask the hiring manager to tell them about the job. Many hiring managers proceed to refer the recruiter right back to the job description they already have. The recruiter just goes through the old job description to make sure it's still accurate. In the end, all you have is a confirmation of what's already in the job description. What if the assumptions made on that job description are wrong? Would that give you good candidates? You're just going down a rabbit hole.

Without a job description, I can ask any question I want. If there is already information laid out for the hiring manager, they are going to default to it because that's what they've been trained to do. They're not bad hiring managers. They're just following directions or following the training they received during previous intake sessions. Without a job description, the line of questioning is going to be very different. It allows us to dig deeper than skills alone.

WHAT TO ASK

Before I get into any details about the role or position, I start by delving into the hiring manager's company and division. The current state of the company may dictate the behaviors needed in a candidate—it's the recruiter's role to figure that out.

First, I ask these three questions:

- Where are you today?
- Where do you want to go?
- What's standing in your way of getting there?

Then I dig deeper into where the company really stands at present. I figure out which of the following stages it's at:

- Is it a "startup," i.e., a new company that doesn't have a lot of established rules, processes, or generally much money for big systems, etc.?
- Is it a "scale-up," i.e., a company that has had some success and growth, and maybe just raised funding from private equity or an institutional investor? Scale-up companies generally need to begin creating policies and procedures to satisfy investors and drive real revenue growth.
- Is it a "grown-up," i.e., a company that's more mature, that has already established rules and guidelines, and is generally more focused on efficiency than real growth?
- Is it a "blow-up," i.e., a company that isn't passing maturity and needs to reinvent itself, a company that's not quite a startup anymore but is in a situation where they need to turn things around?
- Is it a "roll-up," i.e., a company that's focusing on getting bought or merging with another company, usually through a cash-out situation?

All these companies can have the same job description (say, for a controller). But the point is that from a behavioral perspective, the best candidate fit is different for each one. Think about it this way:

- Startup: the best candidate here is likely someone who is used to working very fast, with no rules, and with very little in terms of resources—the kind of person who is comfortable wearing multiple hats just to get things done.

- Scale-up: the best candidate here is likely someone who can bring in processes and understands the needs of investors in terms of reporting, etc.
- Grown-up: the best candidate here is likely someone who is good at finding and solving inefficiencies in large organizations that are often bureaucratic and stuck in their ways.
- Blow-up: the best candidate here is likely someone who's more of a hired gun. They don't mind blowing up everything that exists in order to start from scratch and get it right. After all, there's a big difference between finishing your basement as part of a new construction and remodeling it merely to refinish it—namely, lots more work!
- Roll-up: the best candidate here is likely someone whose focus is short term and generally about the money or another incentive to drive a transaction. Generally, it's about lowering costs to the bare minimum in order to increase profitability on paper and get more for the business.

As you can see, the profile for each of these candidates is *very* different. It makes sense to start there. But most recruiters don't.

The good news is, their blind spots can be your advantage. The first question you need to ask is: what are the three things you need this role to accomplish? There must be specific measurables. You want to know what you're going to measure and how often you're going to measure it. You also want to know the KPIs (key performance indicators) around these items so that you can be clear on the results you're looking for.

When I ask hiring managers about this stuff, they just sit there with a blank look on their faces. I have to tease it out of them. As recruiters and HR professionals, we've been taught to think in terms of skills, not results. Of course, there are some managers who do get it and can easily present their three KPIs, the three things they need done in ninety days, and the eight things they need done in 180 days. You need to be able to do this, too. Having measurable results is the only way to evaluate whether an employee is doing well or not.

Remember: people with different skills can create the same result. If their hearts and heads are in it and they have some basic skills, the rest can follow. By focusing on the results, they will learn the skills necessary to accomplish it. Conversely, a candidate may have all the skills in the world but never achieve the type of results that you're looking for. If that's the case, it probably means there is a disconnect somewhere in the head and the heart.

OVERCOMING OBSTACLES

The second thing you should consider in the intake session is the obstacles that a person is going to face while working toward their three primary objectives. Think about what you want them to achieve and what might stand in their way of achieving these goals. It may be a few obstacles, or it could be several, but whatever the case, every role has obstacles.

We all know there is no perfect position. Establishing this from the get-go helps managers come to grips with the fact that things aren't going to be perfect. It also makes them pay special attention to candidates who have overcome obstacles before. This goes back to the head and the heart.

TRADITIONAL MODELS OF INTERVIEWING

The first process to refine is the recruiter's intake session with the hiring manager. The Results-Based Interviewing™ process is different. Without a proper intake session, you won't be able to do a Results-Based Interview™ because you won't know what you're looking for. You'll default to interviewing for skill.

There are four traditional interview types that aren't results-based:

- **Situational Interview:** Although it isn't used much

anymore, situational interviewing is about hypo-theticals. "What would you do if X were to happen?" This approach was more common in the '90s, but a lot of leaders still use it today. The issue is that the correlation between what someone says they would do versus what they actually do is very low. Candi-dates give the answers that they think you want to hear. Hypotheticals aren't a good indicator of per-formance (with rare exceptions). The only time they become useful is when predicting obstacles.

- **Stress Interview:** This type of interview is usually reserved for high-level positions. The format tries to put pressure on individuals during the interview. For example, there may be deliberate interruptions during the process to see how the executive responds. It puts them in a stressful situation and allows the interviewer to gauge their behaviors and responses. This interview style is not generally recommended for the masses, but it can appear at senior levels.

- **Relational Interview:** These interviews ask ques-tions such as "What do you like most about your job?" and "What charges you up?" While these answers are important to understand preferences driven by the head and the heart, they don't predict performance. I'm not saying it's bad to ask these questions, but you should be aware that this interview style doesn't give any insights on results.

- **Behavioral-Based Interview:** This one is most

closely aligned with Results-Based Interviewing™. The idea is to ask if someone has acted a certain way in a similar situation. If they have, there is a high probability that the candidate will act a certain way again. It's the "tell me about a time when..." type of question.

The issue with behavioral interviewing is we get it wrong 99 percent of the time. This is important to point out because it ties into Results-Based Interviewing™. In behavioral-based interviewing, we have what is called a "tail." The question becomes, "Hey, X, tell me about a time when your organization really pissed off a customer. What did you do to fix it?" Compare that with, "Tell me about a time when your organization really dropped the ball with a customer. What did you do?"

How is that question different from the previous version? The first one leads the interviewee to the desired answer. It doesn't just leave it at "what did you do?" The answer to the broader question may just be that the candidate was relatively new and went to the boss and the boss took care of the problem. It doesn't make it a bad answer. It helps you better understand behavior. But compare that to asking directly, "What did you do to fix it?" The going-to-the-boss answer isn't a viable answer anymore. The person needs to come up with an example of something that they themselves fixed because that is what is specifically being asked.

When a candidate is led to an answer, it becomes a lot easier for them to BS their answers. The interview becomes unreliable because you're not getting a natural response. When you ask someone a very direct question, the answer you get when they don't have a lot of time to think about it is the more natural response. We want to get in the head of the candidate and get past the BS. You can improve your odds by avoiding the tail at all costs!

RESULTS-BASED INTERVIEWING™

Results-Based Interviewing™ ties back to the intake session. The intake session is not about what skills you think you need—it's about what you need to achieve. We want to understand what the candidate has achieved, and if he or she can achieve something similar. It's based on the principle of behavioral-based interviewing, which says if you did something once, you're probably going to do it again.

We are all creatures of habit. If someone can articulate how they achieved a result once, they are likely able to do it again. That's the mindset of a Results-Based Interview™. It's an important distinction.

So how do you carry out Results-Based Interviewing™ to ultimately hit on the head, the heart, and skill? This is the challenge. It's also the part of the Results-Based

Interview that I call The Core Four: Production, Profile, Purpose, and Probe.

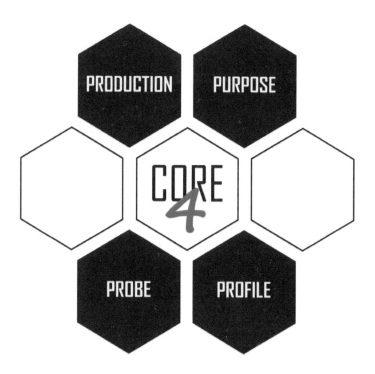

PRODUCTION

In the intake, we outline the specific results we want a position to achieve. The first Core Four concept is *production*. It's all about the results side of things and has four pieces to it. The first piece of production is determining the *objective* for the role and asking targeted questions that help you understand whether the candidate has produced anything similar to the objective.

What are the candidate's accomplishments that are most comparable to the results the hiring manager is looking for?

This could take the shape of something like a senior-level candidate completely reorganizing a company and generating an additional five million dollars in profit their first year. In the interview, you're looking for specific and measurable results. Focus on results first because this opens up the second piece of production: the *outcome*.

The outcome comes from the questions "How did you do that?" and "Why did you act that way?" These questions move beyond skill and get into the territory of head and heart. First, you ask about objective—did they achieve something like this? Second, you ask how they achieved the outcome.

The third piece of production is *obstacles*, which we addressed in the intake. What obstacles do the candidates need to overcome in order to be successful? This would be framed like a behavior-based question where we ask about a time the candidate has dealt with a very similar obstacle. Be mindful not to add a tail to the question, because you want to see if the person has in fact gone through something similar. Again, we are not focusing on skills. These questions are more head- and heart-based.

Finally, the fourth aspect of production is *outlook*. Their outlook is how they tackle problems. Here, it might be OK to employ a hypothetical if the candidate has not been in a situation comparable to the obstacle. This question is geared toward how someone would approach an obstacle, tapping into reasoning or the head. What behavior might they exhibit, regardless of skillset?

PROFILE

The second Core Four concept is *profile*. The profile includes a little bit of the skillset but diminishes the importance of the skills. Instead, it favors the ability to produce results.

A person who produces results is the number one thing you should be looking for.

There are four components to profile: capacity, character, competency, and culture. When it comes to *capacity*, it's quite basic: does the candidate have the skills to do the job? When we ask about capacity, we focus on results first and turn the focus away from just the skills. For example, if you're a programmer, you will need to know how to program in Java. That is a must in order to complete the job.

The second piece around profile is *character*. Have they shown that they want to do the job based on their previous performance? Then comes *competency*: what are the behaviors a person needs in order to be successful at the specific job?

Finally, *culture* hits on the behaviors needed to be successful in the company as a whole. It's all about whether a candidate fits the culture, not just the specific role.

PURPOSE

Core Four *purpose* is also broken down into four pieces: pain, pleasure, pursuit, and the personal. *Pain* is simple enough. What does the candidate currently have in their role that they no longer want? What are they trying to get rid of? Knowing the pain they are currently experiencing helps you understand how the person ticks.

Pleasure is what the candidate currently has in their role that they do like and want to keep around. Generally, these are not financially related. Maybe it's flextime or remote working. It's what a candidate doesn't want to give up because it's important to them. This starts to get into the why behind how the candidate makes decisions.

The third piece is *pursuit*. It's what the candidate doesn't currently have that they are driven to go out and get. This information indicates how they operate deep down, at the level of the heart. What's in the heart will dictate how they act. Which leads into the final aspect of purpose: the personal.

The *personal* describes the absolute needs of the candidates—as opposed to their desires. For example, let's say it comes up that the candidate has a special-needs child at home, and they need to work from home from 9:00 a.m. until noon on Mondays, Wednesdays, and Fridays. It's something that cannot be adjusted. It comes down to a personal situation that can or cannot be accommodated. This, again, hits at what is in the heart of the candidate.

PROBE

The final Core Four idea is *probe*. It's how you ask the questions in each of the previous three Core Four concepts, using four questions:

- *What* are the facts of each situation?
- *Why* are those specific facts important?
- *When* are you going to address this?
- *How* are you going to address it?

As you can see, it starts with the simple question "What are the facts?" without addressing the emotional side; it's just the facts. Then the discussion moves into why those facts are important and when you'd address them. What are the time constraints around them and how are you going to address them?

For example:

- "My boss is a micromanager who makes me check in every day." (*What*)
- "It's important because it shows she doesn't trust me, and I can't work this way." (*Why*)
- "I am going to address this issue within sixty days." (*When*)
- "I am going to speak with her about backing off, or I am going to leave." (*How*)

Whether it's about production, profile, or purpose, you can structure your questions this way to get to the head, the heart, and the skillset around what, why, when, and how. It seems simple because it is. Yet, many people don't do it.

IN THE INTERVIEW

Let's say you're interviewing someone for a role. You start with the objective. Say this role requires the candidate to raise brand awareness by 50 percent in the marketplace. You might ask them to describe a similar accomplishment of theirs. As another example, say the objective is to get on Bloomberg Radio by the end of the year. In that case, you might ask them to describe a situation in which they won their company similar media coverage.

When I was interviewing someone for a head of brand marketing position, I asked the question about raising brand awareness by 50 percent without providing a tail. In other words, in the initial question, I *didn't* ask him, "How did you achieve that?"

As a result, the candidate said his goal was to increase brand awareness by 50 percent, but the candidate was able to achieve only a 35-percent increase in brand exposure with his plan. As a follow up, I asked, "How did you do that, and why did you do it that way?" What's interesting in the original comment is that he admitted he didn't hit 50 percent. He talked about how he hit 35 percent and why. He also laid out what he learned from missing his objective and how he would approach a similar situation in the future.

Next, you address the obstacle question. What is a significant obstacle particular to this role? Maybe it's that the company is short on manpower and didn't start up the brand team the way they should have. Here, you'd ask them to give you an example of a similar situation. After they answer, you might ask them how they figured out a way to get that work done. Why did they do it in a particular way? This unlocks a much more in-depth conversation of what they did, how quickly they did it, why they did it that way, and what the outcome was.

You might then throw in a hypothetical just to tap into the reasoning of the candidate. For example, if the company is short-staffed, how would they approach the situation? It's not just a situational question for the sake of asking situational questions. It's specific to the objective and the obstacles tied to that particular role at that particular company at that particular time.

Chapter Two

MYTH #2: LINKEDIN IS THE END-ALL-BE-ALL SOURCE FOR RECRUITING

It used to be that the response rate from candidates on LinkedIn was 60 to 70 percent. Now it's below 10 percent! What happened? Well, for one thing, it doesn't help that we're all fishing in the same pond. According to many reports, 94 percent of recruiters are on LinkedIn, but I would wager the number is more like 99 percent.

What does it mean that we're all beholden to this same oversaturated source? All too often, we try to compete by carpet-bombing the applicant pool. Day in and day out, we badger candidates with InMails saying, "Hey, I've got a great opportunity for you." Is it any surprise that people don't respond?

Don't get me wrong, LinkedIn *can* work. It can be a helpful tool. But there are other tools as well. It's only *one* option—and most of us are not even using it right.

Why do we waste so much time on it? After all, we know that much of the information people post on their page profiles is highly unreliable. What you see there may not be a flat-out lie, but it is almost certainly, um, *embellished.*

CANDIDATE'S JOB TITLE ON LINKEDIN:

Senior Java Developer
"Looking for my next challenge!"

ACTUAL JOB TITLE:

Barista at Java Cafe
"Looking for on-the-job training."

Bottom line: you don't know who you're recruiting until you actually talk to them.

ALL LINKEDOUT

Think about how LinkedIn operates. It's all a keyword search. As a recruiter, you type in what you're looking for, and if the word is not in somebody's job title or in the body text of their profile, there's a high probability the candidate is not even going to show up. We miss out on some of the best talent this way.

And what about the candidates who *do* show up on the search results? Do we even know how or why LinkedIn is ranking them in the way it does? We do our keyword search and LinkedIn's algorithm serves up a list of candidates according to relevancy. This sounds great on the surface. But how do we know their methods are trustworthy and unbiased? Could it be that the best candidates are being buried on the third or fourth page of results, never to be seen again?

We're not doing ourselves any favors as recruiters by using LinkedIn this way. Even worse, we tend to spam InMail. We reach out to candidates without any thought to how we're coming across. Our words are careless and impersonal.

Let me show you what I mean. Most recruiters use the same basic pitch: "Hey, I've got a great opportunity for you. Saw your LinkedIn profile. This would be perfect for you." Chances are, they know next-to-nothing about the candidates they're reaching out to. They're just using LinkedIn as a glorified database. They haven't spent any time to learn about the person by truly reviewing their profile.

It happened to *me* just a few weeks ago. I had a recruiter reach out about a recruiting job. When you look at my LinkedIn profile, it shows that I own a recruiting firm, that I speak on the subject, and so on. I asked her, "Hey, what was it about my profile that attracted you?" Her answer made it clear she hadn't even looked, and I told her so. That was the end of our conversation, unsurprisingly. But her behavior is indicative of how way too many recruiters use LinkedIn.

When will we learn that spam mailing doesn't work and that candidates *don't like it*?

I know because they tell me. I have reams of data on it. There are even LinkedIn user groups where they bash recruiters for sending them solicitations to positions they are not even remotely qualified for!

I talk to candidates about how they're approached by recruiters, and across the board it's the same feedback: they hate it. They think it's probably an automated bot doing the InMailing, not even a human being. I'm surprised they don't assume we're also trying to impersonate a Nigerian prince and asking them to wire us money!

In all seriousness, we *have* to stop blasting people this way.

Recruiters: enough with the spam. Enough with the "InMail and pray."

MISSING KEY INFORMATION

LinkedIn wants you to do everything within their platform. Their business model wants you to continue to come back to the site repeatedly. If you search for a position such as a VP of Service Delivery for Company A, you'll get a few results one day and then a few repeats and different results the next day. They do this because they want you to have to come back to LinkedIn and live within it—even hold you hostage to it.

For example, Kirk is the VP of Service Delivery for one of my companies, Qualigence International. If you searched for his exact title and company in LinkedIn, he wouldn't show up in the search results. But if you knew his full name and searched, it would pop up right away with the exact title. From a recruiting perspective this is strange, because the algorithm wasn't serving us up what we really wanted, even when using exact keywords. Yet, it gave us names immediately.

This seems kind of stupid because if we knew someone's name already, why would we use LinkedIn in the first place? In our minds, when we use LinkedIn we think we get access to everybody, but that's not how they deliver information.

HOW TO USE LINKEDIN AS A RECRUITER

People need to understand that LinkedIn is a great tool, but it has its limitations. There are some really superstar executives and tech folks on LinkedIn, but a lot of people end up getting buried. So how should we use LinkedIn?

Let's say I'm a recruiter filling roles in finance. I can't just keep going back to the well of people in finance and spamming them the same messages. Instead, I need to get involved in the user communities. There are a gazillion and one groups to choose from and users can be involved in up to fifty of them. In these forums, you can start to comment on other's posts and build credibility as a real source of value. It's a way to prove you're actually subject matter savvy in particular spaces. When you establish more credibility, potential candidates are more likely to respond to you.

Volume isn't everything. Instead of spamming one hundred people, do some research and InMail ten of the right people. Google their names and research them to see if they have written anything or won any awards. It shows that you've done some background research and due diligence on candidates. In a nutshell, it shows you genuinely care.

It's also very important to consider your approach when reaching out to someone. The wrong thing to do is to send the "Hey, I've got a great opportunity for you!" email. Instead, say something along the lines of "Hey, I saw this on your profile" or "I found this on Google" and emphasize that you want to know more about them as a person and the next steps they foresee in their career. Generic spam messages are all about the recruiter; this individualized approach is all about the candidate.

When the focus of attention shifts away from the recruiter, we see response rates go from 10 percent to over 60 percent. Often, I don't have to spend much time at all on recruiting because my response rates hover around 80 to 90 percent. In this industry, a sniper shot is more effective than a shotgun blast. If you're methodical about your approach, you can get what you need while still living within LinkedIn.

USING ENDORSEMENTS THE RIGHT WAY

I don't put too much value on endorsements on LinkedIn. They are usually just a collection of someone's friends or acquaintances, and they don't tell you much. However, since professionals are often connected to others in the same industry, endorsements are a great source of additional candidates!

Instead of using endorsements to vet someone's expertise, use them to broaden your pool of potential candidates. Look at the people who have endorsed your potential candidate. There is a high probability those individuals fit the same keywords but may have not come up in your search. Reach out to those endorsers. Recruiters miss this source of opportunities all the time.

Years ago, it was common for candidates to list three or four references at the bottom of their résumés. Often, we made more hires based on those references than the actual résumés themselves. Now, keep in mind that references are different than endorsements. Endorsements are most often done without even thinking. In fact, I have endorsements where I don't even know where they come from! But references, or referrals, usually come from people we know. They are much more meaningful. It takes a little extra work to get good references and a lot of people aren't willing to put in that effort. Recruiters assume LinkedIn knows best about what they need and don't go further than that. But if people are your biggest asset, why would you settle for automated LinkedIn search results?

A ROBUST PROFILE

When it comes down to it, a recruiter cannot be haphazard about anything. If you are a recruiter on LinkedIn, you need to build out your profile to make sure you are just as credible as the candidates you wish to hire. Think about it: if you reach out to somebody on LinkedIn, what's the first thing they're going to do? They're going to look at *your* profile.

Most recruiters tend to be very generic in their profiles. They take an approach like "I'm the recruiting god. I do everything." Yet, that's not necessarily what candidates want to see. If you're recruiting within the finance space, a candidate is going to want to see that you've got expertise in the field. Your profile must reflect this.

Profiles are also useful for finding the right titles that you're looking for. A lot of titles are ambiguous or vary from company to company. On the left-hand side on the bottom of the candidate's page, LinkedIn gives you alternative titles to look for that are related to that person's profile. This is a good place to search. So many recruiters never even get there. If you're beholden to one tool, you sure as hell better know how to get everything out of that tool!

BEYOND LINKEDIN

Although LinkedIn is the default candidate-sourcing tool at this point, there are hundreds of other tools out there. Some of them are free; others are paid. Obviously, they're not *all* essential. But there are a few things as a recruiter that you absolutely have to know how to do or you're selling yourself short.

One of the most basic tools is a Boolean search on Google. This lets you draw from LinkedIn and other sources. Making the most out of your searches is Recruiting 101, but it's shocking how many recruiters don't know how to use Boolean operators such as parentheses, quotation marks, and ORs and ANDs. There is so much information available online and learning the basics of Google keyword searches opens up the ability to tap sources outside of LinkedIn. Google now uses natural language processing or NLP to help with these searches, but it doesn't replace the targeted accuracy of Boolean searches.

Most organizations don't properly train recruiters on the tools available to them. When a recruiter for a corporate entity is hired, they are told to use job boards and LinkedIn along with an applicant tracking system, and that's it. Can you believe it? That's the extent of the training most organizations give recruiters. To be a skilled recruiter, you must use a variety of tools: you have to understand how to leverage Boolean searches, how to make the most of GitHub, and how to do a Facebook timeline search. Recruiters with these skillsets are few and far between.

DATA SCRAPERS

There are some very useful tools in the form of data scrapers. These tools scrape web pages, industry sites, conference sites, and so on for contact information. These spiders will reach out and continue to scrape up any relevant data that is in the public domain. There are a ton of them, but one of the more popular ones is called Data Miner. It has many applications, but essentially it scrapes up the good stuff from the immense amount of information on the web.

Since emails and phone numbers are often redacted or hidden on LinkedIn, recruiters often resort to using InMail to contact potential candidates. Data scrubbers can pull up extra contact information for a candidate. Be aware that these tools are not always 100-percent accurate. They might give you an old phone number or email address, but often you can find ways to reach a potential candidate outside of InMail. Since people usually ignore or immediately delete their InMail messages, having an alternate contact point helps boost response rates.

Text messages currently have the highest response rate over any other method of recruiting. There are even a bunch of paid and free text-messaging tools such as Textio. If you scrape enough information, you can contact people right at their phones and use a third party so your personal number isn't being used. You get a dedicated number that can be changed at any time for the candidate to respond to!

Social media account marketing is another useful tool to employ. You can set up Google alerts and plug in specific keywords to alert you to profiles that include those words in Facebook, Twitter, Instagram, and other social media platforms. There are even image-related searches that find names attached to specific images. While this is not a common way to find candidates, it can be a useful tool to find people in more creative careers.

Of course, not all information gathered by scrapers and keywords is going to be relevant. You don't want to drown in thousands of names. It's your job as a recruiter to pare things down. The mindset of too many recruiters is finding as many potential candidates as possible for the top of the funnel. They don't think about how to get them out of the bottom of the funnel. The more effective strategy is to target a smaller, more relevant population of professionals and reach out to them in the right way and at the right time. Make this your mantra.

ANALOG

So far, all the tools we've covered are digital tools. They're not enough to get you everyone that you need. Take, for example, recruiters looking to hire nurses: a lot of nurses aren't on LinkedIn or Facebook communities. In these cases, you can buy a directory of contact information of every nurse in the state. For many industries, this old-school approach can connect recruiters to the right people.

Lists of conference attendees are great analog tools, and it can be useful to sponsor a conference for this reason. Attendees on these lists are often grouped by their professions. Groups of people who are licensed by state—such as truck drivers, doctors, lawyers, and so on—can be accessed for small fees. You want to have access to as close to 100 percent of the population as you can. Even though the majority of them are online, the more tools you use, the closer you can get to that number.

REFERRALS

As mentioned earlier, one of the biggest and most overlooked sources of information comes from referrals. It seems simple, but most of the rock star recruiters get to a point where most of their business comes through referrals. The success of this approach goes back to how recruiters reach out to people.

It's a common mistake to send the "I've got this wonderful opportunity!" email, followed up with "Do you know anyone who might be interested?" I don't have to explain to you again why this is the wrong approach. You know by now that your correspondence with potential candidates should focus on *them*—the people you're approaching. You want to know more about the next steps in their career, assuming there are some.

If your first potential candidate wasn't a good fit, they may very well point you to someone who is. People generally like to help others if the request is presented in the right way. Connecting with candidates is about building relationships, and with better relationships comes the likelihood of referrals. A good way to frame a referral request is to say, "Based on your profile and our conversation, if you were in my shoes, who are the two people you would call today for this role?" This question doesn't guarantee success, but it starts another line of thinking regardless of whether the person knows anyone who is interested.

When you consistently ask for referrals, you open the door to someone saying, "You know what? I don't know if this person's going to be interested, but I would call Sue." Now you've got the opportunity to call Sue at someone's referral. This isn't just an old-school way of networking; it's a classic tool that has always been there, and a lot of recruiters don't know how to do it. Their loss. I know of several recruiters today, internally and externally, whose entire practices are built on referrals. Whether you're a corporate or agency recruiter, you should be making this a regular practice.

Being a good recruiter is about checking in every so often. You don't want to be emailing people once a year. By then, they will have forgotten about you. Check in every three months, especially the first year. This is where technology becomes useful. You can have prewritten emails that can be distributed automatically that ask how people are doing and set up future contact. Continuing the communication is key.

Furthermore, if someone enjoys the work they are doing at a company, they're likely to refer their friends and family. If they are unhappy, then they may potentially point you in the direction of someone who might be looking to leave a bad situation. Again, you need to switch the focus from what you need as a recruiter to what the other person needs.

Take the example of a *Fortune* 100 company that offered a $2,500 bonus to employees per referral if the new hire lasted ninety days in the position. This approach wasn't working, so they upped the bonus to $5,000 per referral. It was still cheaper than using a recruiting service, but the boost lasted only a few weeks and then it dropped off again. They then raised the bonus to $7,500 and again saw the same result.

Later on, a new head of talent acquisition moved in and refused to pay these huge fees per referral and capped them off at $1,000. All of a sudden, they started getting more referrals from the current employees. What did they do differently?

We think throwing money at a problem is going to fix it, but that's not always the case. Financial reward *did* help for a while. But what really made the difference here was when the company made asking for and giving referrals a part of its DNA. They spoke about it at every company meeting, referenced it in every company-wide email, and celebrated it in every staff meeting.

If you're not engaging your employees to drive referrals, you're wasting a lot of money that's right under your nose. Although it seems counterintuitive, the most successful referral programs are usually the ones that pay the least amounts of money. This effect happens precisely because these companies don't lean on monetary compensation. They know it's about more than just the money.

USING YOUR OWN APPLICATION TRACKING SYSTEM

Let's follow the experience of a candidate who is going to apply to one of the big advertising agencies. First of all, the candidate has no idea who is receiving their application because the agency uses an application tracking system, or ATS. As a result, the candidate's name and information are attached to a specific job.

The candidate doesn't have access to a recruiter's contact information because the recruiters hide behind the ATS. Instead, the candidate gets automated emails. The recruiter gets the internal notification that 200 people applied for a job, and then they do a keyword search in the system to find the best ten to fifteen applicants. Then they'll flip through the résumés and pick four or five people that they'll reach out to. That's usually it for the process.

If the candidate in our example doesn't make it past these filters, they either get no notification, or they get a standard "Dear John" letter saying thank you for the application, but the company will be going in another direction.

The candidate's information is now in the company's database, but it's attached to a specific position. But what if that position was too senior for the candidate's application? What if they are better qualified for another position? Although they're in the system, most recruiters won't do a search to find this candidate because their information is attached to the wrong job.

Every *Fortune* 1000 company has this problem. They're sitting on a gold mine of people but do nothing with them unless those candidates apply for a specific job. All it takes for these *Fortune* 1000 companies to find this talent is to do a Boolean search in their own system. It's funny because it seems like common sense to search for the free stuff that you already own, but recruiters aren't trained to source this way.

Recruiters make the mistake of assuming that if an applicant doesn't keep reapplying to jobs, it means that they are not interested or they got hired elsewhere. That's a fallacy. Instead of mining the contact information from past applications, recruiters are taught to go straight to the tools that they have licenses for such as CareerBuilder, Monster, Indeed, LinkedIn, etc.

A bigger issue is that it isn't easy to search for candidates already in most ATSs. Although search ability can be a technology issue, usually it's just that many companies don't search their own databases. I've been hired by companies where I found many of the candidates I needed by scrubbing their own database. It's mind-boggling that corporations don't pick up on this.

Over the past twenty years that I've been assisting companies with recruiting, I've developed a mantra that goes like this: *I want you to do it right first. If you get to a point where you can't, I have access to resources you don't that will help.* I always encourage companies to use this iterative process. First, you use the stuff you already own because it's free. Second, you use the stuff you already own because you paid for it. Third, if you don't own it, you go find it. And last, when you've exhausted your options, you do the most expensive thing and seek an agency's help. Of course, by the time I teach people this, they've already called in an agency to help: they've called me. But that's the point. That's how strongly I feel about it: I show them all the resources that will help them avoid having to call me in the future.

CHOOSING THE RIGHT SOURCE

Companies should use an iterative process when it comes to sourcing, but they often don't. For example, LinkedIn is a very good source for recruiting salespeople. They are on LinkedIn because they use it for business development themselves, and they tend to respond well to recruiters. So LinkedIn becomes a source for hiring that type of candidate.

However, when it comes to tech people, recruiters should consider a tool like GitHub, which is where most tech people can be found. If, for example, a company needs a Python developer, they can turn to GitHub because candidates have a place to post their code there.

To be clear, no single tool is the best for searching all industries. The key is to match the job profile with the best tool for that category.

Take the example of a large coffee chain that created a sourcing portal for all their recruiters. They can go into the portal and search for, say, a mid-level finance person at a specific comp level and area. They can pull up a list of 150 tools—prioritized by position, location, and level—that have helped source candidates in the past. But most people don't approach sourcing that way. They keep going back to the defaults and hope to find what they need in there.

Even though it doesn't seem like it, there are so many tools out there, beyond LinkedIn, that can be used. But there's no silver bullet, so exploring other options such as GitHub, social media, and non-social media platforms is imperative. Data Miner is a fantastic scraping tool. Textio is fantastic for texting potential candidates. Email Extractor is great for finding people's emails. MailTester can validate emails to make sure it's a valid address. There are also other databases such as ZoomInfo. What it boils down to is hitting quality versus quantity.

Why is this important? Recruiters complain about not having enough time to recruit for all their roles that they already have and end up creating more work by spreading very broad wings. Instead, they need to focus on quality. A good recruiter can learn to recruit for any role. However, the more a recruiter specializes in a functional area, the more credibility they have when they reach out to candidates. People can sense the recruiter's level of familiarity in an industry right away.

If a candidate for a programming position can recognize that a recruiter doesn't know the difference, for example, between a Java and a Python developer, it can come off as downright offensive. Two years ago, I knew a recruiter who took on a client that specified in their intake that they wanted a person with ten years of experience programming in Python. The recruiter emailed people until they got a candidate on the phone who told them they had only four years of experience in Python. The candidate also said that they were about the best the recruiter was going to find.

The recruiter was a little dumbfounded at the candidate's answer until the candidate informed the recruiter that Python started only about four-and-a-half years previously! The recruiter had done no research, and his resulting mistake was pretty embarrassing. It's not often a candidate knows more than a corporate recruiter because of the recruiter's failure to ask the right questions.

I'm not saying everybody has to be a subject matter expert, but they should at least know how to do a Google search and become subject matter savvy. That's the minimum that good recruiters must do. Truly, a good recruiter must spend the necessary time doing research. If they are going to make a convincing case and get a quality candidate, they need to know what they're getting into.

Chapter Three

MYTH #3: RECRUITERS DON'T NEED TO BE MARKETERS

In the past, there were eight to ten applicants for every available position. Nowadays, according to the Bureau of Labor and Statistics, there are actually more open positions than there are unemployed workers. To make things worse, it seems that less than 3 or 4 percent of available candidates are even qualified for the jobs they are applying for!

As recruiters, we must think about how we market ourselves to the communities we recruit from. Looking at recruiters' activity on social media, it feels like 90 percent of recruiters spend their time marketing to each other instead of those they are trying to recruit. There are tons of recruiter groups on Facebook and LinkedIn filled with corporate and third-party recruiters. They post nonstop, sometimes fifty to sixty times a day, about what they're doing, their gripes, or to share good ideas.

Many of these recruiters are extremely active within these insular groups. But when it comes to actual recruiting, few are participating in the groups that include the actual people they are trying to recruit. So what's the point?

It's great to belong to recruiting groups and share trade secrets and best practices, but if you already see the value of giving to industry groups, why wouldn't you do the same for the groups you're trying to recruit? Recruiters use these platforms as glorified databases when they are much more than that. It isn't rocket science; it's fricking Marketing 101.

A MATTER OF SURVIVAL

When you ask recruiters about how they are marketing themselves and what marketing tools they're using, they look at you with these big eyes and say, "I'm not a marketer. I'm a recruiter." I always think, *Are you kidding me?*

In this day and age, we all need to be marketers to make

up for the shortage of qualified candidates. We need to get in front of people the right way. It's a simple and inevitable fact that if you're not a marketer, you will become extinct in the near future.

THE WRONG MINDSET

There are many people in these recruiting groups for recruiters who are going on about how unemployment is at an all-time low and yet they can't find enough clients or candidates. They are primarily third-party recruiters who complain that they don't have enough positions to work on and few companies are coming to them. This is a theme that keeps popping up: *companies aren't coming to me; candidates aren't coming to me.* Could it be because the recruiters aren't using their time to market themselves and instead are spending way too much time complaining in these industry user groups?

People need to spend their time building their credibility as experts in their respective recruiting fields rather than hiding in chat rooms or private user groups. For some reason, many recruiters don't think that way.

Corporate recruiters also tend to hide themselves and their contact information online. The rationale is understandable: you don't want people calling and emailing you and clogging up your inbox. But there are ways around that. You can create folders where certain emails go and to which you can respond when you're ready. You can set up automated responses that say, "Thanks for reaching out." These kinds of responses at least look like two-way communication, and they provide some value and acknowledgment.

All too often, recruiters just don't respond to people and then find themselves calling these same people when they find them on LinkedIn later on. They're asking people for a favor, but they don't even respond to emails. It's become way too selfish, which leads to a horrible candidate experience.

BASIC CONTENT MARKETING

Recruiters must understand this isn't the "Have I got a deal for you!" marketing from twenty years ago. It's about *content* marketing. What's the purpose of content marketing? It's to provide value and build credibility.

If you're marketing a software tool to a financial services industry, are you just going to pitch the software? No, you're going to provide value to the industry by creating relevant content regarding technology innovations, industry trends, and so on. Then, when you call on this community or a need comes up, guess who it is that they remember? The people like you who provided real value.

For example, I have more than twenty years of experience recruiting in financial services and have even served as a bank board member. As a result, I can have meaningful two-way conversations with people and make relevant and informative comments on forum discussions. These moments aren't about recruiting. Instead, people see that I am engaging with their day-to-day business. They see that I know what I'm talking about. When they look at my profile, they see more than just a recruiter looking to fill a role. At this point, they are more inclined to reach out to me if they are looking to hire someone because they see that I know banking.

It comes back to what recruiters fail to do so often, which is to be customer and candidate focused. Recruiters are always asking for help from the community but not contributing to the community. It's all one way. It's all "I need you." That's not how marketing works. You can't keep blindly sending InMails and praying for responses. That's just doing the same thing and expecting different results—which is one of the definitions of insanity.

IDENTIFYING PAIN POINTS

If you're going to market to someone beyond content marketing, you have to figure out what their pains are. You have to focus on addressing and providing a solution for those pains. It's not about the recruiter; it's about learning a customer's motivations before you pitch anything to them. In marketing, this is called understanding candidate personas.

When I was recruiting for an anti-money-laundering position at a bank, I went to LinkedIn and found some prospects. But I didn't reach out to them. I didn't reach out because I had no credibility in this specific field—yet. It was the first anti-money-laundering search I had done.

Instead, I read through several anti-money-laundering groups and threads and was able to pick up on trends, current roles, and government regulations that were hot topics. When I reached out to the people I was targeting, I asked them about how some of these trends were affecting their roles. Notably, I didn't just say, "Hey, I've got this great opportunity I'm trying to recruit you for."

By opening up dialogue, I was indirectly giving back to the community and validating that I knew about their specialty. Looking for trends is what marketing companies do. They want to know who is saying what about specific products so products can be positioned the right way. Recruiters have to do the same.

Sometimes it can be as simple as showing interest and being a willing learner. When I was recruiting for a software development position, instead of going in all elbows,

I went in saying I'd like to learn more about software development. I'd ask questions unrelated to any job. The people on the forums loved to train each other, so they were very willing to help me understand the nuances in app development and other areas.

I kept the dialogue up for a couple of weeks, and when I came back with the question, "Hey, if you guys were hiring for somebody with this skillset, where would you go to find them?"—everyone came out of the woodwork. I made multiple placements out of this one user group because I had invested the proper time and energy researching and developing relationships. If I had just tried recruiting off the bat, they would have kicked me out of the group! In fact, a lot of tech groups refer to recruiters as "trolls," because they rarely provide any real value.

Recruiters need to put in the work. They need to initiate conversation and be willing learners and listeners. It's time to really listen and not just wait to talk! Yes, it requires a little more time and energy, but the rewards are huge. You have to build your brand, and this is where you start.

WHAT'S YOUR BRAND?

In most cases, recruiters aren't taught that they are their own brand. They're taught that they work for this big company and that brand stands on its own. There is some truth to that. For example, it's easier to recruit for Starbucks than it is for Joe Schmo's Coffee Shop around the corner. But the thing recruiters forget is that they are the ones reaching out, not Starbucks.

Recruiters need to distinguish themselves by developing their own brands. Most recruiters are afraid to open up and put their contact information out there. They're taught they shouldn't release their email or phone number or else they'll end up with a full and unmanageable inbox. While there is some truth to that, there are ways to manage it. You can automate certain aspects. You don't have to respond to every single inquiry. There are all kinds of solutions, but most recruiters want to hide. They have the mindset that they're just recruiters. They don't need a brand.

That mindset must be reframed. It's not saying, "I'm a Starbucks recruiter." It's saying, "I am a recruiter who happens to work with Starbucks, but here's what I do. My focus is on supply chain and logistics. I've spent the last eight years recruiting and helping Starbucks build out their supply chain and logistics organization." What a difference, right?

Now, when that person reaches out to someone, their reputation precedes them. They are now the "supply chain expert." A person they encounter could be interested in Starbucks or maybe in the competition. But no matter what, they will see on LinkedIn that this recruiter is the supply chain guy and a credible source.

Perhaps the brand Starbucks helps in certain areas, but it may not be so significant in others. If brand didn't matter, then we'd all just hire a bunch of telemarketers to do recruiting. Unfortunately, many recruiters spend a majority of their time on online forums whining about their hiring managers or about not having enough candidates. How does this help build a brand?

BRAND BUILDING

When building up your brand, there are a few things that need to be considered. First, you need to make sure your LinkedIn and social media profiles support a certain brand and message. Your profiles shouldn't stop with your title and the company you work for; include what you do and the value you bring people within specific skill areas or functions. Point to the articles you've written on those topics. This all has to be accessible so you can build a following and connect with people.

Second, anything you put out on social media must be consistent with your brand message. You can't just be posting about what you had for lunch. You have to post about trending topics and employ the correct hashtags related to a specific industry. You have to post about candidates you've successfully placed. Ask these candidates to make recommendations on LinkedIn with comments, rather than stop with a simple and meaningless endorsement.

In this way, you can start building momentum to show your expertise on, say, supply chain and supply chain recruiting. People will stumble across the information and hashtags you use, and from there, they can see your presence and brand. This takes time and consistency. Without this, you'll remain unknown like any other recruiter.

TONE IN MESSAGING

As we've seen before, there are grave errors in the tone of messaging that many recruiters employ. A lot of them come off as impersonal or even bot-like. They oversell because they know nothing about the candidates. It's flattery gone awry and a whole lot of *me, me, me.*

Messaging needs to be focused on the customer. It's Marketing 101, but recruiters don't think about it. Recruiters need to be aware of the pains and trends in whichever industry they're appealing to, and their messaging needs to reflect that. Their messaging needs to contain information that can help solve that pain.

When you reach out to a targeted candidate, you shouldn't start by selling them on a role. You don't even know yet if they're the right fit! So rather than giving the candidate everything you think they need to know about the job up front, focus on opening communication. The initial contact should be about building a relationship. It should have the singular goal of getting someone to respond and start a conversation.

Often, initial contact attempts are too long, give too much information, and give the person the opportunity to say no right away. If the message is short and sweet and about the other person, it's more likely that person will respond. Recruiters must express interest in learning more about someone and their motivations. People love to talk about themselves, and that needs to be leveraged; don't just pitch a job and hope it sticks.

One key approach is to simply tell the truth. As a recruiter, I very likely don't know anything about the person I am trying to recruit. Why lie and pretend like I do? If I try to get to know a potential candidate, there's a higher probability they'll respond.

Another approach is to spend time on social media to uncover trends and challenges within the industry you're targeting. Using this information, you then engage professionals in the field. For example, I once reached out to a VP of digital marketing about a position at an insurance company that was very old-school in terms of marketing. The insurance company was having a hard time getting people to respond to them because they weren't known as a progressive company.

In this particular organization, the head of digital marketing was going to have their own technology and development team. This is rather unusual for the industry. As a result, my approach to recruiting was to ask potential candidates how they managed the disconnect between digital marketing and technology. People responded well to this question because it was a common issue. As a result, my response rate from initial outreach was in excess of 75 percent because I made it about the other person. I wove in what I knew about the roles instead of blindly reaching out.

As recruiters, we need to know how to listen so we can learn. We have to be able to solve problems, but to solve the problems, we also need to know what those problems are. Recruiters can look to salespeople as models: it's consistently true, across industries, that 20 percent of salespeople make 80 percent of the money. It's because that 20 percent spend the time building their brand and doing the proper research, instead of just trying to sell something.

PERSONALIZATION

I am a big fan of leveraging automation in certain aspects of messaging. When done correctly, it helps save time and energy. Still, a lot of people don't realize that automated messages can be personalized, too. It can be as simple as merging the candidate's name, title, and current company strategically into messages and turning the focus onto the person. With smaller pools and senior-level candidates, automation isn't as effective. You should be dedicating much more time toward understanding your target and creating a highly personalized message.

I understand that many recruiters may not feel like they're the best writers. But this is really just a cop-out. Too many times, salespeople and recruiters think they have to use big words, eliminate contractions, and make sure everything is perfect grammatically. They're overthinking it.

Personalization is about writing like you speak. Now, that doesn't give you the green light to use swear words and be sloppy, but you also don't have to get caught up trying to appease all the grammar Nazis out there. Sometimes, using all caps and bolding certain phrases actually gets a better response rate because it looks different from a canned paragraph. People don't like reading long, boring paragraphs. They prefer bullet points. You need to frame things in a way that compels action. It needs to feel natural and unforced. A great reference for recruiters is *How to Write Copy that Sells* by Ray Edwards.

Personalization also depends on your audience. If you're going after a CFO at a *Fortune* 500 company, they will tend to be a little more buttoned up and professional. While you'll have to adjust your tone, it should still reflect the way you actually speak. If you get on the phone with a candidate and you sound very different from your written message, it may come off as disappointing.

HOW WE BUY

As humans, we buy emotionally and justify rationally. It's a common experience to go to a store, fall in love with a pair of shoes, drop $500 on them, and then go home and wonder why you paid so much for those shoes. It's precisely because of that emotional attachment. It's because we looked damn good in the shoes and that's the emotional response we seek.

Similarly, candidates will buy into a position emotionally and justify the change later. All too often, recruiters start with the rational: title, compensation, job duties, etc. Marketers, on the other hand, know to start with emotions. They've been doing it for years. It's how Apple gets us to spend $1,200 on the new iPhone. They place the product in the frame of "why" we should buy it and not "what" we should buy. Apple sells us on changing the status quo, being different, and challenging the industry. As a result, the customer feels that they are actually cooler because they have an iPhone. It's tied to our emotion, not practicality. Otherwise, we'd buy the cheaper Android.

When it comes to recruiting, the traditional approach is to start with the job description. It's all very practical. What if you started instead with something like, "Hey, I know the pain you're feeling in this role because in most organizations, technology and digital marketing are separate and it raises the following issues..." This approach identifies the pain points that an individual is feeling and aims to help solve them. There is no discussion of the nuts and bolts of the job. Instead, it focuses on the *context* of what's going on in the industry and the position.

The change in approach is about changing how you position the opportunity. As a recruiter, you're trying to sell all kinds of jobs. You want to know what makes the candidate tick and what pains they are feeling so you can discover their emotional drivers. You don't want to come across as a used-car salesman and convince someone they have problems that they don't. Instead, you want to gain agreement on a problem that already exists and try to address that problem. These problems usually start with emotion and end with a practical action.

Recruiters must start with people, identify the industry problem that everybody recognizes, and then identify the pains or emotions attached to that problem. After that, we need to think about the ripple effect because of that problem. What other issues does the problem potentially cause? We try to find out ways that these pain points can be resolved and we consider the possibility of certain solutions. Don't say your position is the solution; ask the candidate to consider the possibility that there is a solution.

When we've identified possible solutions, we present to the emotional side, the pleasure—again, this is because we buy in emotionally and justify rationally. After addressing the candidate's need for pleasure, it's time to paint a path to this potential pleasure through conversation about a particular organization or position. We all know it's never easy for someone to change jobs or think about the practical aspects of employment. That's why we must first uncover the candidate's emotional drivers and then present the opportunity in a way that addresses those emotions.

Chapter Four

MYTH #4: CANDIDATES ARE ONLY INTERESTED IN TITLES AND MONEY

We all know that in the recruiting industry we're supposed to focus on the motivation of the candidate. The reality is, we don't. Researchers have uncovered that the majority of recruiters focus their attention on a couple of specific bits of information within a candidate's résumé: education and current title. Then they half-ass their review of the rest of the résumé.

Recruiters and managers continually fail to focus on anything else in terms of competency. They're spending six seconds per résumé before deciding on the viability of the candidate. The majority of them spend less than ten minutes preparing for interviews. In most cases, they're looking at a résumé while running into the interview. They aren't prepared to ask the right questions that uncover behaviors and motivations. They know motivation is key, but they default to stated skills and titles on a piece of paper.

COMMON MISCONCEPTIONS

People invent all kinds of titles these days. If we look at a résumé for a director's job, we automatically discount the candidate if their title is "VP." The error is that we assume two things: we think because they're a VP, they won't take a step back; and we assume money will be an issue because we can't afford a VP.

This is an error because compensation varies wildly from company to company, even with the same positions and titles. Recruiters are making decisions *for* people without talking to people, and they're basing those decisions on the assumption that what matters to the candidate is money and title (extrinsic motivators), not intrinsic motivation.

Yes, money and title are important. But if a candidate's intrinsic motivations are met, these extrinsic items take second stage.

The other assumption we make is a more generational one. Although all generations have stereotypes, there is a negative perception about millennials in particular. The assumption is that all millennials want beanbag chairs, big titles, flex hours, and keys to a new BMW. Assumptions like this are dangerous and, as the saying goes, can make an ass out of you and me!

I have two millennial children who couldn't be more different—not only from each other but also from the traditional perceptions of millennials. That said, they defy the stereotypes in very different ways. If I were recruiting them and made the typical assumptions about their generation, I wouldn't be able to connect with or recruit either one.

RECRUITER RELATIONSHIPS

To many recruiters, candidates are a commodity. Without a proper relationship, when asked what drives them, over 70 percent of candidates just tell recruiters what they want to hear, not the truth.

Sometimes what recruiters want to hear and what candidates say line up, but often they don't. Of course, recruiters want to hear that a candidate solved every problem they've ever dealt with. So that's what they're going to hear. Without doing the job of connecting with the candidate and building a relationship, we can't expect to hear answers that are completely truthful.

Let's say a candidate *does* care about their title but says that they don't. Or perhaps a candidate indicates their primary driver is money. Usually, when a candidate cites money and title as primary drivers, they're not lying—who doesn't want to be paid more? They're being honest in their own mind. Yet, all too often it comes down to the candidate feeling that they're not getting paid enough to put up with all the bullshit they're dealing with in their current role. So is money the cause or the effect? Is it correlation or causation?

Recruiters stop short when figuring out the real motivations. Recruiters think it's all about titles and money because they've heard it so many times. Ideally, they should go digging to uncover what's driving that motivation around money. Sure, for a limited number of the population it is purely about money for money's sake. Money is important to all of us, but statistically, it's not the number one reason we accept or decline a position. Candidates and employees often say, "I don't get paid enough to deal with this bullshit!" Well, if they could get a job without the bullshit and headaches, they might not place so much value on a higher salary. They wrongly assume every available job is that frustrating, so they insist on being paid more. It takes some work and leveraging positive communication to reveal this deeper meaning behind their desire for higher pay.

As mentioned in chapter 1, Results-Based Interviewing™ gives you the map to identify the real drivers each candidate has. Digging deeper through probing questions is critical at this stage.

You don't want to invalidate someone who may think money is their biggest driver. You start a conversation around the *what,* which is they don't feel they're getting paid enough. The second question considers the *why.* Why do they think they're not getting paid enough? The conversation will usually reveal the candidate's needs: they feel they've taken on more responsibility than they're being paid for, or they don't have support in their role. In my experience, 90 percent of candidates will relate some other issue to the reason why they think money is the issue.

Inevitably, there is a small percentage of candidates for whom it truly is all about the money. They may be drowning in debt for whatever reason and are only thinking about dollars. This is also indicative of some other factor in their environment affecting their judgment.

APPLYING CORE FOUR QUESTIONS

We know it's not all about the money. We know it's not all about the title. Often, those individual concerns point to problems that everyone in an organization is experiencing. We need to dig deeper and ask the questions that reveal whether it's really about title and money or something else under the hood.

Once we identify that a candidate thinks they're getting underpaid for this or that reason, the third question is always about the *when*. When do they anticipate addressing this core problem? Not the money problem, but the actual problem that's causing the pain. Have they tried to address it? Are they going to address it? Are they giving themselves thirty days to fix the problem? It helps a recruiter understand how big of a deal the problem is to the candidate.

The fourth question is always about the *how*. How are they going to fix the issue? It could be "I'm going to quit" or "I'm taking a job elsewhere." It could be a host of things. Those are the big four questions I use over and over: What is it? Why is it? When is it? And how is it?

It's not rocket science. Most recruiters just stop short. We make the dangerous assumption that it's about money and a title for everybody.

THE FIVE PS

Recruiters tend to treat candidates like commodities. We get a position and we look to fill it as fast as possible. We make the conversation with candidates all about what we want as opposed to what the candidate wants. Because of this, we think about people in three pieces: knowledge, skills, and abilities. It's why we look at résumés. We get an idea about them and make decisions based on that.

But we cannot forget that there's also the head and the heart. The heart is the intrinsic motivation or how we're wired because of our beliefs. The head is how we behave based on those intrinsic motivations. This is what we really need to figure out. To do this, we use the five Ps: Purpose, Person, People, Profession, and Profits.

Everybody is motivated by the five Ps, but everybody's Ps are different. Recruiters tend to assume everybody's Ps are the same, but it's our job to figure out what drives a candidate based on those Ps.

- **Purpose:** Everybody has what I refer to as faith and focus. Faith is the system of beliefs, experiences, and environmental factors that ultimately drive the focus of your life. In order to really understand a candidate, we have to unpack this. What's their purpose in life? What drives their decision making?
- **Person:** This is how people look at themselves. I break

it into two pieces: fitness and fuel. Do they take care of themselves physically? What about mentally? Certain drivers of behavior come out in the workplace based on how people take care of themselves. If they cannot take care of themselves, then they can't take care of others. If they don't take care of themselves, they tend to have a negative outlook on life, which might change the things that drive them. Does their behavior in this regard align with their purpose and who they are?

- **People:** The third P is really about family and friends. People like to talk about a work-life balance, but I see it more as a work-life blend. When my son had football games for his high school team, I made sure I was home to see them. It's what mattered to me. A person's relationships with their family and friends affect the types of jobs they look for. I've seen people take pay cuts so they could spend more time with their kids. Understanding how people look at those around them illuminates intrinsic motivations.

- **Profession:** Every candidate has specific thoughts and ideas attached to who they are as a professional and what they want to become. The key is understanding not just where they are, but also what they want to achieve and *why*. The *why* is the key!

- **Profits:** We can't discount the importance of money. When it comes to money, we have our financials and freedom. Financials are the target amount someone needs or desires to make. The key questions to answer are, what is the amount, and what's the plan to get there? Freedom is driven by each person's primary drivers. Does freedom mean the ability to buy a big house? Or does freedom come in the form of taking every Friday afternoon off to attend a child sporting event?

Money is important, but there is a whole range of other factors that we have to dig into to really understand a candidate and see where their drive comes from. Get into those five Ps and you can start to uncover who a person is and how they make decisions. Over 90 percent of the time, it's not only about the money.

Understanding candidates in this deeper way is not just important to hiring but also to retention. Usually, recruiting is very front-end, but it shouldn't stop the day the new hire starts. Once you understand all of someone's intrinsic drivers, it pays to stay with them, because not all people fit into roles. When an employee fails, it often occurs during the first eighteen months. It might be because they were motivated by the wrong things, or because they were a bad candidate. The question to consider is, *were they dead when you hired them, or did you kill them?*

Usually, we put people into jobs and we don't pay attention to their intrinsic needs. Later, someone offers them $2 more per hour and they leave. It looks like it's all about the money, but really, it's because we weren't focused on retention. If people are happy where they are, that won't happen as often.

Furthermore, an employee's success or failure goes beyond the alignment between a person and their role. Sometimes you've got the right person in the right role, but they've got the wrong team or the wrong manager. This often prompts an employee to leave for the next company that offers to pay them more.

MOVING FORWARD

Recruiters keep doing the same things over and over again and expecting a different result. It's crazy. I know because I've done it myself. I've made every bad hiring decision you could possibly think of. I've reprimanded and fired the wrong people. I've done everything the wrong way in the past. But I've learned from those mistakes, and that's why I know how and why to do things differently.

We need to change our process in order to improve as recruiters. Looking at a résumé or a LinkedIn profile for a few seconds is not enough. A candidate's title or schooling doesn't predict performance at all. We need to start looking at what they do. What candidates highlight on their résumés is generally what they are passionate about.

Look at what candidates have accomplished and relate that to the role you have. Don't discount them because they didn't go to Harvard. It takes a little more time to read between the lines and get the gist of what really drives someone.

We also have to better prepare for interviews. So many people just walk in and ask candidates to explain their résumé. Tell me about your last job. What did you do there? Why did you leave? Those are important questions, but there is no structure behind it. We need to prepare by writing down the very specific what, why, when, and how questions based on what we uncover. If you have several insightful questions prepared, a candidate will know you're more interested in them. And if the candidate feels valued, they'll give you more information about what drives them. If recruiters want to stop hearing the answers candidates think we want to hear, we need to stop winging it and prepare for interviews. We tend to present jobs as perfect scenarios that the candidate should be honored to join. There's little authenticity in that. Guards go up and it only leads to surface information.

Conversations need to be more genuine. Organizations need to acknowledge that they aren't perfect and that there are issues that need to be resolved. Being authentic about challenges that candidates will have to face is a way to get closer to their real drivers. People are hesitant with recruiters because it seems like they are always being sold a role. People can't be authentic when you're blowing smoke up their butt.

There are no perfect companies—not Google, not Apple, nor anybody else. People appreciate authenticity and usually become more interested in a role if you're honest. It also gets people to respond in a more authentic way. Trust me. It will make your job as a recruiter so much easier.

Chapter Five

MYTH #5: RECRUITERS ARE NOT RESPONSIBLE FOR THE QUALITY OF A HIRE

A little while back, I encountered a peculiar coincidence that shed some light on the disconnect between business leaders and recruiters when it comes to finding quality candidates. I was sitting in my main office in Michigan when I got a call from a guy who whispered into the phone, "Hey, is this Steven?" I said, "Yes, who is this?" But before I could answer, I heard the shuffle of paper and a door closing, and the guy hung up. I was left just thinking *what the hell was that?*

A week later, I was on a flight to Florida and I struck up a conversation with the guy sitting next to me on the plane. He happened to be the CEO at a local tier-one auto supplier and shared that he was heading to Florida to check on the progress of his 16,000-square-foot "retirement" home! Obviously, the guy did really well for himself. He then politely asked why I was heading to Florida. I told him I was doing a talk at an HR and recruiting conference, at which point he recoiled in his seat, leaned away, and said, "Oh, you're one of them!"

I asked him what he meant. With a look of disdain on his face, he said, "You're probably like all of the other HR people and recruiters that I've dealt with." I again asked him to please clarify what he meant, and he went on about how he had this head of HR and recruiting who gave him all this great data on how many hires they had each month and the cost of those hires—but no dates on their performances. In fact, this CEO made it clear that most of the people his company was hiring fell well short of performance expectations. He clearly blamed the lack of quality on the candidates being recruited and presented by his HR and recruiting team.

We had a long discussion about his frustration and perspective. But when the plane landed, we went on our merry ways. I delivered my keynote at the recruiting conference and successfully returned home—but couldn't get the encounter out of my head! About a week later, I was again sitting in my office and guess who called me back? I recognized the voice because it was that same whispering voice that had hung up on me a few weeks prior. He said he was the head of HR and recruiting for a local tier-one automotive supplier and that he had a big issue. His team was filling positions quickly and inexpensively, but the CEO was all over his ass. He was talking about the same CEO I had sat next to on the plane the previous week! After realizing the coincidence, we chatted a little and I told him about my encounter with his boss.

A couple of weeks later, I was invited in to meet with them to better understand their recruiting and retention challenges. The CEO was blaming HR for presenting poor-quality candidates to his business leaders and felt they were being forced to select from the bottom of the barrel. He wanted better quality. The HR leader argued that his team was providing quality, but the hiring managers were making the bad decisions. They had a disconnect between the perceived quality of their hires and who was ultimately responsible for fixing the situation. While this is just one company, it's far from an isolated incidence. I can assure you it happens all the time in businesses, and you may have experienced something similar at your company.

CHANGING PERSPECTIVES

My philosophy is that there should be a minimum standard, or bar, every candidate must meet for an HR or recruiting team member to present them to the hiring manager. Anybody above that bar should be a quality candidate who fits the profile, culture, and character that the hiring manager needs. It's not a foolproof system, but it leads to a high likelihood of a quality candidate.

The fact is, as recruiters, we want hiring managers to select from the candidates we put in front of them. But what if they end up with the best of the worst? They compare who they have because they need to fill the role, instead of comparing each candidate to the minimum bar! This seemed to be what was happening with this auto supplier. The CEO even admitted that he had hired individuals who probably didn't meet the bar, because that's all that was put in front of him to choose from.

A lot of people in the industry might disagree, but HR and recruiting professionals are more than just initial matchmakers. I try to get them to look at it differently because it's a great opportunity for a recruiter to increase the overall quality of their candidates. The hiring process ultimately impacts the performance of their business. It doesn't just become about putting a butt in a seat; hiring the right person becomes *the* game changer.

A lot of people love to blame HR and recruiting. We are a whipping post. That's also precisely why the industry doesn't want to take ownership of the quality of candidates. Do they actually hire the person? No. Can they influence a hiring manager's selection? Without a doubt, and good recruiters and HR staff usually do. We have the ability to influence, which is a lot of power to wield.

PROPER METRICS

There is a saying that goes something like this: what gets measured gets done. Part of the problem we see in the world of recruiting comes back to what data we are measuring and which metrics take priority. The two most commonly used metrics are time to fill a position and cost per hire.

When it comes to time to fill, we measure how long it took for the recruiter to identify, recruit, and place a new employee. Cost per hire measures the cost to fill the role. Did I use an agency? Did I have to pay for an ad to get posted on a social media platform? Whether I'm a corporate or agency recruiter, that's part of my performance. It's hammered into us.

These days, so many companies talk about quality of hire, yet all they measure is time and cost. If that's all you're measuring, you're sending a message (and not a good one) about what you think is important. Moreover, if you *talk* about quality but measure activity, that sends a confusing and hypocritical message to the recruiters driving the process.

The point is, if you're not measuring the quality of a hire, guess what? You're not going to get quality.

Furthermore, when bonuses—or other recognition and reporting—are based on time-to-fill and cost-per-hire metrics, it causes other problems. There's no accountability for quality, yet we are holding recruiters responsible for quality. It's a bit unfair to put recruiters in that spot.

The way recruiting success is measured is not going to change overnight, but we can begin to place more weight on quality. We don't want to scrap metrics like time to fill because if it deteriorates from 30 to 180 days, that's a problem. Still, we must keep the end goal in mind. We are trying to find the right person in the right role for the right team, for the right boss, and for the right company. We need to put more emphasis on the activity that gets us there.

PERFORMANCE-BASED METRICS

It's difficult to measure the quality of new hires when we are not clear on the specific objectives of the role. If we can't measure it, how do we communicate specific accountabilities to the new employee? How do they know if they are meeting expectations or failing miserably? It is imperative to define specific, measurable, attainable, and relevant metrics for specific 60-, 90-, or 180-day time frames. If the hiring manager and new team member are clear from day one on what is measured, then you can rate that employee's performance against those goals and based on real data.

The first argument I get with this is that sometimes the hiring manager can just be a jerk, the kind of person who runs through candidates. While there may be some truth to that, it's on you to identify this pattern. You can't just push it off and blame the hiring manager. Part of your job is to find the right cultural fit for that hiring leader as well as for the position. If your manager is that big of an issue, it's time to have an honest conversation with them, your HR partner, or even the hiring leader's boss!

We tend to focus on skills and abilities when talking to both candidates and hiring managers. We really need to address the head and the heart in order to find people who fit the position, the team, the manager, and the company. You're doing a hiring manager a disservice whenever you put a candidate in front of them who shouldn't be there in the first place. Without putting into practice the process we've discussed so far, it's going to be very difficult, if not impossible, to gauge the quality of candidates.

It's not just about a good or bad candidate. It's a good candidate or a bad candidate for a particular position, a particular manager, a particular group, company, etc. Those considerations create a much deeper discussion of what it means to make a successful hire at your company.

CREATING OBJECTIVES

You can't measure quality if you don't know what quality is. Every employee who comes into your organization, from the secretary to the top salesperson, should have clear, measurable objectives. Yet, most companies don't do this. We must teach our managers and the rest of HR how to create the right measures and expectations before they hire a new employee. We must establish the measurable KPI, what's in our control, how we're going to measure performance, and how often.

It can be a tedious process. A lot of companies don't have performance management systems, or PMSs. A PMS can take all that data from candidates and store it in one place where it's easily reported on. If I'm placing hundreds of people at my company year-round, it's going to be relatively hard to find all that information manually. As a recruiter, we have to work with our HR counterparts on logical ways to get this data. We need this performance information to measure if we're doing the job we need to. Are we bringing in the quality an organization needs?

This mindset change is crucial, but it's not easy due to how cemented recruiter mindsets usually are. They focus on activity, not performance—because they have been trained to! This shift will require untraining that mindset, and there will be major pushback.

This could be a golden opportunity for every recruiter to jump on a quality- and performance-centered mindset and champion it in their organization. We have to embrace the fact that we can make or break a company based on the people we give our managers to hire. It's what makes recruiting exciting. But we also have to present it with confidence or else we get crushed at the door.

SELLING WITH CONFIDENCE

There are a couple of different ways of presenting candidates to hiring managers. What if I, as a recruiter, have developed three candidates and have spent hours with these people on the phone or in person to get into their drivers, and then I just email over the résumés to the hiring manager? I've done all the homework, but I haven't really communicated any of the information to the hiring manager about the candidate beyond what's on the résumé.

This is a common yet avoidable mistake. By not properly presenting the whole candidate, the hiring manager may assume I know nothing about them. Why shouldn't hiring managers think this? How does this affect the quality of the hire?

In this scenario, the hiring manager must decide whom to interview solely based on a résumé. For that reason, I need to get on the phone with the hiring manager and clearly explain how the candidate meets the minimum bar. For example: *Candidate A exceeds that bar in this way. This is what they achieved, and this is how they did it. This is why I really like them.* Think about how much more responsive the hiring manager will be if they know what drives a candidate and why they're a fit.

Even though it does take more work, I've seen this approach succeed over and over again. CEOs who previously had strained relationships with HR and recruiting have changed their tone. First, candidates were presented in a more complete light. Second, executive conversations changed. They started to focus on performance of business as a result of the work accomplished in recruiting. The conversation wasn't just about cost to fill or hire time. It was about performance and the immediate impact the candidate could have on the business.

Years after working with one company to change their recruiting culture, the head of HR invited me to lunch just to show me printouts of the company's stock prices, before and directly after we started working with them. He wanted me to see the direct relationship between the success of the business and their new focus on bringing in better hires, not just volume of hires.

We need to change the approach. We used to present and pray. Now we must present a whole picture of someone in the right light. It holds you accountable for making sure candidates hit the minimum bar and the hiring manager understands that you've spent the proper time with the candidates. When recruiters take the time to do this, hiring managers are more willing to listen and to build relationships. With better relationships between hiring managers and recruiters, you can strongly influence their decisions. Now you can make a real impact on the company.

Chapter Six

MYTH #6: RECRUITERS WILL BE REPLACED BY TECHNOLOGY

Recently, I was leading the search for a senior vice president for a client. We're talking $275,000 per year in salary, plus bonus, equity, and a whole host of other executive perks. As part of the search, I reached out to a senior executive who was employed by one of the Disney companies. If you know anything about Disney, once people are in, they tend to stay. But I figured what the hell. Why not give it a try?

After I left a voice mail message, I got a call back from this candidate in less than twenty-four hours. This is what he told me: "The past ten to fifteen years, a lot of recruiters have reached out to me, but most of them seem to be through automated emails. I know that technology is infiltrating everything, but you're one of the few people who actually took the time to call me."

Technology is a great tool, but it won't replace good recruiters. The question of how technology is changing recruiting is a hot topic right now. In the past, I'd get call lists. I would place an ad in the paper. I'd have to sift through hundreds, if not thousands, of résumés. The sheer volume of contacts wasted a lot of time. Then we started automating a lot of the processes. Sites like Monster and CareerBuilder moved to the forefront saying that they'd solve all our recruiting problems.

Of course, at this point a bunch of recruiters ran for the hills. But did it erase recruiters? No. So what happened?

In fact, it created more work for recruiters because job boards were being populated with so many candidates. It was easier for them to apply and thus easier for recruiters to market to more people. Companies hired more recruiters to screen and sift through the sheer volume of applicants. Recruiters weren't replaced.

LEVERAGING TECHNOLOGY

People tend to freak out about the unknowns of the future. After Google's AI made a phone call to make restaurant reservations, people started worrying about which human beings this creepy technology was going to replace. In the same way, recruiters worry that computers will soon be able to talk to candidates. Let's evaluate the positives and negatives within that.

Most recruiters spend a lot of time on repetitive tasks. Many are on LinkedIn all day long clicking through candidates and sending out InMails and emails. Automating some of these mundane processes seems like a good thing. It eliminates a particularly repetitive task that a computer can do faster than a human (since we are often searching based on keywords).

Although there are some "auto-matching" technologies that exist, computers still can't figure out what to look for on their own. The computer will do what we tell it to do, but as recruiters, we have to evaluate the results. Sure, a computer can match some candidates via keywords and titles, but can you really rely on these data points? Are you going to hire someone just based on what's on their résumé or LinkedIn profile? Of course not! Plus, do you remember the biggest complaint candidates have when going through a heavily automated process? It's impersonal. Nobody is getting to know them. They don't have anyone to reach out to.

A big topic in recruiting these days is candidate experience. This relatively new idea is not as new as we think. Businesses have been focusing on the customer experience for centuries—how come it just hit recruiting in the past few decades?

If you go on sites like Glassdoor, people can anonymously bitch about companies, the interview process, the interviewer, their experience with the organization, etc. These negative reviews, many of which may not even be true, are turning off other candidates from applying. This problem can't be fixed through technology. It can only be fixed through developing one-on-one relationships.

There is an opportunity for recruiters to leverage technology so they spend less time on repetitive tasks that can be automated. This allows them to spend more quality time with candidates and hiring leaders. Artificial intelligence can't fix a broken process. Technology can't replace a recruiter. Smart, tech-savvy recruiters are going to be the rock stars of the future!

Until people start saying, "I don't want to deal with another human being," we're OK. I don't think we're wired to want to eliminate the human aspect. But a recruiter has got to embrace technology or risk being left behind.

DON'T MAKE THE PROBLEM WORSE

Think about a company like Amazon. They have state-of-the-art processes and distribution systems. They leverage technology throughout their entire organization. Often, when they introduce new technologies, it's less about fixing a problem and more about creating efficiencies. Amazon is by far the leader in distribution and logistics. They already have a system that works, so when they add technologies, it just gets better and better.

But if your system is broken, then adding technology will only make things worse. If there are inherent problems in your recruiting process, speeding up the process through technology will only make you fail faster! If your process is not built with a focus on quality, adding technologies just speeds up the process of throwing crap at a hiring manager.

Recruiting organizations are notorious for what I call the silver bullet syndrome. We see a new technology as a silver bullet without understanding how it fits into what we're doing and what the ultimate cost is. There's a difference between using a technology just because your neighbor is and thinking about whether your process is actually working and where technology can create efficiencies.

KEEPING UP

Recruiters have to run a delicate balance when it comes to employing technology. On the one hand, it's imprudent to introduce technology too fast. On the flip side, you never want to fall behind the times. If you want to stay in business, you can't hide behind the phone all day and keep calling people for the next forty years. You need to look at how to leverage technology the right way.

Not long ago, the internal recruiting group for a *Fortune* 500 client was struggling to meet the recruiting needs for customer service. Each recruiter was carrying between thirty and forty open positions at a given time. The total open positions were more than 25 percent of the employee base of the division. Feeling significant pain due to the open role, the business unit leader demanded the recruiting team find more candidates, much faster, and at any cost.

After reviewing multiple options, the organization invested more than $150,000 in a software platform that leveraged artificial intelligence to scrape the web for potential candidates, automatically message them, and even respond to their inquiries. The platform was cutting edge and, as you can imagine, very flashy.

But three months after deploying this massively expensive platform, there was little improvement in the number of positions filled by the recruiting team. With actual expenses topping out at over $165,000, the president of the business was furious. I remember the business unit president screaming at his internal recruiting group, asking, "What the hell is going on? I spent $150,000 on technology that isn't changing anything. We're not getting better, and we're sure not getting more candidates."

After a review of their recruiting processes, technologies, assessments, etc., I quickly determined that their problem was never based on a lack of candidate volume. In fact, this new technology was causing an even bigger bottleneck. Why was that? Because it turns out their internal interviewing and vetting process was the real culprit. Instead of fixing a perceived volume problem through technology, they caused an even larger overload on an already crumbling system.

At this point, instead of using technology to get more candidates, they reassigned the money for use on a different technology platform that helped them vet candidates faster through online videos and assessment tools. Their mistake was that they initially viewed their problem as a lack of input. In reality, the problem was that their system was not designed for throughput. Automating their broken process only created a more glaring issue.

Happily, these days the company is seeing more than

twice the candidate flow as before, and open positions have dropped to less than 5 percent of this particular workforce population.

This all points to the fact that you can't just throw money at a problem or invest in a technology without understanding the problem you're trying to fix. You need to focus on the right aspects of a process to support a business with technology. If you can figure out how to leverage technology to your benefit, it will make you indispensable as a recruiter. You'll be working more efficiently while maintaining the right structure and mindset. You'll be making an impact that the people and organization can feel.

CONCLUSION

YOU ARE THE KEY

There are multiple big decisions you make in life: where you go to school, whom you marry, the house you buy, and whether or not to have kids. Many of these decisions are influenced by your specific career choices. You, as a recruiter, impact people's lives in a very big way because you are directly influencing many of these life decisions.

If you do it right, not only do you help companies perform better, but you also make a significant impact on the individuals you place. The potential impact you have on those you recruit is probably much bigger than you have previously considered. Once you understand your responsibility to get recruiting right and leverage that perspective every day in your role, it will fundamentally change your approach to your work.

Many recruiters just get it wrong. It's not just candidates and companies who feel these pain points; recruiters do, too. If we say people are our greatest asset, let's actually treat them as such. Sure, we should automate where it makes sense, but we can't automate our relationships with hiring managers and candidates. Spend the proper amount of time really getting to know the people you are working with and recruiting.

It's time to stop buying into the myths that have held the recruiting industry back for so long. You now have a road map—which you can begin to follow right now—that will have a massive impact on your organization and the people you bring into your business.

Now it's up to you. It's time to reevaluate your mindset and start applying the principles found in this book. It's never too soon: you can begin doing this tomorrow. Wait, I take that back. You can start *today*.

ONE LAST STORY

Les is the head of talent acquisition for a large, publicly held organization in the information technology industry. With more than twenty-five years of experience and having led recruiting and sourcing teams of more than 500, Les knows recruiting. Or so he thought.

Les and I were having dinner one evening when he shared with me that he had lost his drive and that his boss was ready to fire him. After more than two decades, Les felt that there just wasn't anything more he could do to improve his team, their results, or the ratings they received from their internal customers. Les was getting bored, and it showed.

Just for kicks, I gave Les an incomplete copy of this book to review, with one condition. He had to be honest with himself and with me regarding how he approached each myth. A few nights later, Les called me at about 11:15 p.m. and was fired up. He was like the Energizer Bunny on steroids as he described example after example of how he fell into the trap of believing many of these myths. He also talked about all the new initiatives he was planning to roll out to his team to break free of the traps that they found themselves in.

Like all of us in recruiting (myself included!), Les and his team are still on a journey. According to him, the myth-busting lessons they learned from this book have already made a significant impact on not only them but also the businesses they support and candidates they come in contact with. He is thrilled with the progress they've made and wants to keep going.

Now, it's your turn!

ABOUT THE AUTHOR

STEVE LOWISZ is a recruiting industry veteran and talent optimization guru with more than two decades of experience helping companies find and unlock the performance of their teams. He is an expert on talent acquisition, talent assessment, talent engagement, diversity and inclusion, and business performance, which has allowed him to serve hundreds of organizations and thousands of individuals across the globe. As the CEO and founder of the Qualigence Group of Companies, Steve regularly contributes to industry events and publications and has been featured in Fortune magazine, CNN Money, and the Detroit Free Press, as well as on Bloomberg Radio.